# BRITISH RAILWAYS

## PAST and PRESENT

## No 44

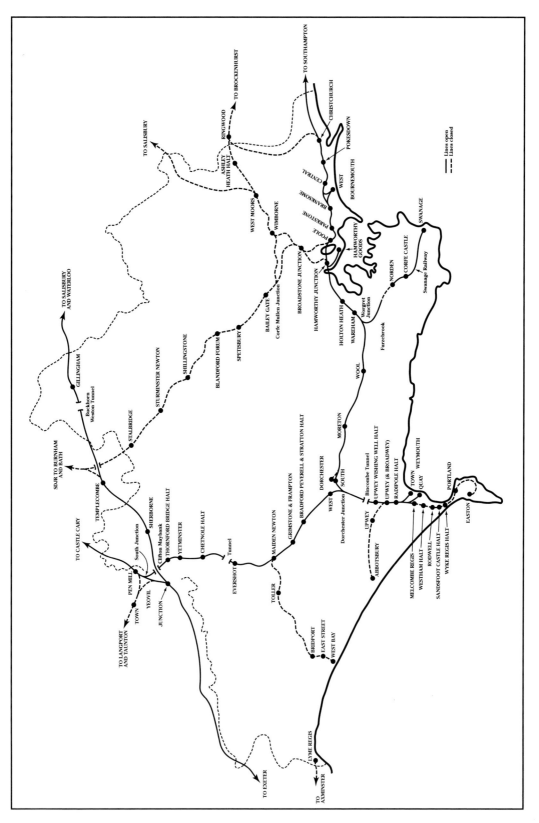

Map of the area covered by this book, showing locations featured or referred to in the text.

# BRITISH RAILWAYS

# PAST and PRESENT

# No 44

## Dorset
## Part 2

### Terry Gough & David Mitchell

Past & Present Publishing Ltd

First published in 2004

British Library Cataloguing in Publication Data

A catalogue record for this book is available from the British Library.

ISBN 1 85895 219 0

Past & Present Publishing Ltd
The Trundle
Ringstead Road
Great Addington
Kettering
Northants NN14 4BW

Tel/Fax: 01536 330588
email: sales@nostalgiacollection.com
Website: www.nostalgiacollection.com

Printed and bound in Great Britain

All tickets and luggage labels are from Terry Gough's collection.

**CLIFTON MAYBANK: Type 3 Hymek No D7045 is at Clifton Maybank with a Weymouth train on 11 April 1966; the line has just been singled. The Yeovil Junction to Pen Mill line can be seen in the left distance.**

**On 9 October 1994 Class 37 No 37414 *Cathays C&W Works 1846-1993* heads the 09.00 Bristol Temple Meads to Weymouth train. This was normally a summer-only working, but continued to run for a few weeks into the winter timetable.** *Ronald Lumber/TG*

# CONTENTS

# BIBLIOGRAPHY

Beale, Gerry *The Weymouth Harbour Tramway in the Steam Era* (Wild Swan Publications Ltd, 2001) ISBN 1 874103 674

Gough, Terry *Rediscovering Railways: Hampshire, the south of the county* (Past & Present Publishing, 2000) ISBN 1 85895 168 2

*The Southern Railway Collection: Hampshire and Dorset* (Silver Link Publishing, 2003) ISBN 1 85794 136 5

*The Southern Railway Collection: The West Country* (Silver Link Publishing, 1999) ISBN 1 85794 135 7

Gough, Terry and Mitchell, David *British Railways Past & Present No 29: Dorset* (Past & Present Publishing, 1996) ISBN 1 85895 089 9

Mitchell, David *British Railways Past & Present No 8: Devon* (Past & Present Publishing, 1996) ISBN 1 85895 058 9

*British Railways Past & Present No 30: Somerset* (Past & Present Publishing, 1996) ISBN 1 85895 089 0

Phillips, Derek *The Story of the Westbury to Weymouth Line* (Oxford Publishing Co, 1994) ISBN 0 86093 514 0

Roose, Graham and Ballantyne, Hugh *British Railways Past & Present No 22: Wiltshire* (Past & Present Publishing, 1994) ISBN 1 85895 049 X

**MAIDEN NEWTON: A down freight hauled by '2800' Class No 3803 waits for the road at Maiden Newton on 7 June 1958.**

   The view from the end of the platform in July 2002 finds Class 31 No 31159 approaching on the 16.20 service from Weymouth to Westbury. Despite running every Saturday in mid-summer, this train (and the outward working) did not appear in the National Rail Timetable. *R. M. Casserley/TG*

# INTRODUCTION

In this, the authors' second book depicting 'past and present' photographs of the railways of Dorset, we have tried wherever possible to include locations not previously covered. Inevitably we have included many stations shown in our previous book, but with different views and, of course, with any changes since 1996.

We anticipated that the few remaining locomotive-hauled trains shown in our first book would no longer be running. There has, however, been a most welcome but unexpected re-introduction of locomotive-hauled trains on the Westbury to Weymouth service, which is likely to continue for the near future. Locomotive-hauled trains were also running into Weymouth from the Southern main line when we began preparation of this book, but have since ceased. New rolling-stock has been introduced, including the 'Voyager' diesel multiple units (DMUs) and 'Desiro' electric multiple units (EMUs), the latter signalling the end for BR slam-door electric trains. Refurbishment of second-generation DMUs has also taken place, with significantly improved interiors, but with liveries more appropriate to buses than trains; perhaps this is a reflection of the origins of the train operating company concerned. All this has meant that we have been able to show more variety of trains than expected. Wherever possible we have given greater coverage to more interesting trains, against the commonly used stock.

Dorset is a mixture of large towns, particularly along the coast, and villages, which make up much of the west and north of the county. This is reflected in the nature of the railway stations. Bournemouth had two stations, Central and West, the latter closing in 1965. Central is now known as plain Bournemouth and is well situated near the town centre. Bournemouth has a population of 151,000 and neighbouring Poole a little less. In addition to the resident population, visitors descend on Bournemouth by the tens of thousand for holidays. There are on average four arrivals in each direction per hour during daytime. By contrast, Thornford is a request stop with a two-coach-length platform between Dorchester and Yeovil Pen Mill and serves two small villages, each about 10 minutes walk away and with a combined population of less than 1,000; it has eight trains per day. The station is known by some rail users as Thornford International, but the local bus company has, for the first time in decades, referred to it in its 2003 timetables as Thornford Bridge Halt, a name dropped by British Railways a quarter of a century ago. The nearby Local Authority road sign, also erected in 2003, calls the station Thornford Halt. Even Thornford attracts passengers on leisure trips, as it is used by individual ramblers and those on guided walks. The numbers are very small, but nonetheless welcome. Such is the variety found in Dorset.

Dorset is served by several train operating companies. Services from Waterloo to both Weymouth and Yeovil Junction are provided by South West Trains. Bristol to Weymouth trains were until recently operated by Wales & West, but are now run by Wessex Trains. Trains from the Midlands and North are operated by Virgin Trains. First Great Western occasionally encroaches, but only at Yeovil Junction on West of England trains when its main line is closed between Castle Cary and Exeter. The Swanage Railway provides seasonal services from Swanage to Norden, and in the future hopes to connect with South West Trains at Wareham.

There is very little freight traffic in Dorset, the only regular services being operated by English, Welsh & Scottish Railways (EWS) to Hamworthy for scrap metal and aggregates, Wool for sand, and Furzebrook for liquid petroleum gas; the latter is due to cease running at the end of 2004. At Yeovil Junction the South West Main Line Steam Company has excellent facilities for the servicing and turning of steam engines, which arrive from the West of England main line or the Bristol to Weymouth line. Although the Somerset & Dorset Joint Railway (SDJR) between Bournemouth and Bath has gone for ever, there is activity at Shillingstone where there is a project to restore the station and surrounding area to its 1960s appearance. The Bristol to Weymouth line is promoted by the Heart of Wessex Rail Partnership.

Traditionally the county has seen seasonal rail traffic. There were large numbers of scheduled and special trains during the summer, for example from the Midlands to Bournemouth via the SDJR and to Weymouth via Westbury. The last remnant of this was, until 2002, the Virgin Trains Saturday-only service to Weymouth via Reading and Basingstoke. Virgin Trains no longer operates west of Bournemouth. The only remaining significant difference between summer and winter services is on the Bristol to Weymouth line on Sundays, when in the summer there are six trains in each direction, whereas in winter there is half that number.

Access to sites for the present-day equivalent views is in many cases becoming increasingly difficult. The lineside between Clifton Maybank and the former county boundary near Yeovil Pen Mill is almost impossible to reach, as it is now densely wooded. Other places have become out of bounds by virtue of redevelopment. One surprise to the authors was that at Buckhorn Weston, on the Waterloo to Exeter line, the western end of the tunnel, which for decades could not be seen from the nearest public access point, was cleared of trees in 2002 and excellent views are once again possible. One aspect that has not changed and for which the authors are most grateful, is the continuing willingness of landowners to allow access to their premises for photography.

**Terry Gough, Sherborne**
**David Mitchell, Exeter**

# ACKNOWLEDGEMENTS

The authors thank the various photographers who have kindly loaned us material for this book. We also thank the proprietors of Classic Pictures of Christchurch for the provision of some of the early photographs. We are grateful to British Railways for granting lineside access for the 'past' views, and the staff of South West Trains and Wessex Trains for help with the 'present' views at operational locations. We thank Colin Pattle and Dick Ware for information on present practice.

# Weymouth to Yeovil Pen Mill (exclusive)

WEYMOUTH (1): On 6 July 1961 two BR Standard locomotives are on passenger trains, bound for Bristol on the left and Bournemouth on the right.

The present-day view shows clearly the extent to which the station has been reduced in size. The remaining platforms are on the extreme left between the coaches and the row of terraced houses. *H. C. Casserley/TG*

**WEYMOUTH (2): Rather a low-key building for the terminus of a main line from London, this is the frontage of Weymouth station on 18 June 1979.**
   **A new station was opened in the summer of 1986, but the new station building has even more limited facilities, not sufficient to cope with the crowds of people travelling by train in holiday periods.** *DHM/TG*

WEYMOUTH (3): On 15 September 1987 Class 33 No 33113 is leaving the station with empty Class 438 (4-TC) unit No 8022. It will reverse this unit into the next platform and attach to unit No 8029 and Class 33 No 33110, which will form the 13.32 service to Waterloo. The conductor rail is in place pending electrification.

On 27 June 1998 Class 58 No 58047, with 58039 on the other end of the train, works the 'Wessex Wanderer', which had left Worksop at 06.05. *Both DHM*

**WEYMOUTH (4): Class 117 DMU No B450 arrives at its destination forming the 12.00 service from Swindon on 26 May 1987.**

**Little has changed here, as seen in the April 1995 photograph showing Class 158 No 158825 forming the 11.00 service to Bristol Temple Meads.** *Both TG*

WEYMOUTH (5): Although some of the sidings have been removed, there is still plenty of activity as Class 33 No 33113 shunts Class 438 (4-TC) unit No 8022 after the latter had arrived behind No 33118 as the 08.32 service from Waterloo on 15 September 1987. These formations were operated in push-pull mode, mainly over the unelectrified section from Bournemouth.

Class 31 Nos 31459 *Cerberus* and 31602 *Chimaera* pass the same point as they berth the stock from the 09.30 from Westbury on its first day of operation in July 2002. Most of the sidings have been taken up and buildings erected on the land. The view is partially blocked by encroaching vegetation. *DHM/TG*

*Opposite* **WEYMOUTH (6):** The 15.51 semi-fast Weymouth to Waterloo train passes the site of the entrance to the engine sheds on the right, with Class 33 No 33115 at the rear of unit No 8026 of Class 438 (4-TC) on 26 May 1987.

On 20 July 2002 Class 31 Nos 31459 and 31602 are seen again, working the 09.30 service from Westbury. The sidings on the left are still in use. *Both TG*

*This page* **WEYMOUTH SHED:** The importance of Weymouth is amply demonstrated by this view of the engine sheds with its array of Bulleid 'Pacifics' (Nos 34023 *Blackmore Vale*, 35013 *Blue Funnel* and 34024 *Tamar Valley* being watered) and BR Standard locomotives, including No 76005, even as late as April 1967.

By the time that the second photograph was taken in August 1970, all this had been swept away, and the shed site was subsequently used for housing, as seen in the 'present' view. *Ronald Lumber/ Barry Thirlwall/TG*

RADIPOLE HALT, with typical GWR waiting huts, is seen looking towards Weymouth in the 1950s.

Virgin trains introduced the 'Voyager' units in the summer of 2002 on a Saturday-only Weymouth to Manchester Piccadilly service. These trains only ran until the beginning of the winter timetable, with Virgin's announcement that it would in future not run any trains further west than Bournemouth. This is the first train to be operated by a 'Voyager' from Weymouth, which ran on 8 June 2002. *Lens of Sutton/TG*

**UPWEY & BROADWEY: Standard Class 5MT No 73085 passes through the station with the 4.43pm stopping train from Weymouth to Bristol Temple Meads on 6 August 1966.**

**On 19 December 2002 Class 150 No 150236 works the 11.02 service from Weymouth to Bristol Temple Meads into the station, which is now called plain Upwey (previously there had been a station of this name on the Abbotsbury branch).** *Ronald Lumber/TG*

**UPWEY BANK: A BR Standard Class 5 assists 'West Country' Class No 34021 *Dartmoor* as they climb Upwey Bank with the 5.35pm Weymouth to Waterloo train in August 1966.**

Photographers still flock to Upwey Bank when there is a steam special running from Weymouth. By way of contrast, this photograph shows two-coach Stores and Sandite EMU No 930030 descending the bank on 15 October 1994. These coaches were formerly of Class 416 (2-EPB), built in 1954/55. *Lawrence Golden/TG*

UPWEY WISHING WELL HALT: 'Battle of Britain' Class No 34071 *601 Squadron* climbs past Upwey Wishing Well Halt on the 3.50pm service to Waterloo in June 1966. The platforms are still in good order, despite the halt having closed nine years previously.

On 13 May 1995 Class 442 No 2406 glides past the site of the halt forming the 15.48 service from Weymouth to Waterloo. This calls at all stations to Poole and major stations thereafter. *Both TG*

**BINCOMBE TUNNEL: Class 4MT No 76018 and 'Merchant Navy' No 35017 *Belgian Marine* approach Bincombe Tunnel with the 5.50pm from Weymouth to Waterloo on 8 July 1956.**

**In August 2002 a Virgin 'Voyager' Class 220 passes the same point forming the 09.10 service from Liverpool. The return working terminated at Manchester rather than Liverpool.** *Peter W. Gray/TG*

**DORCHESTER JUNCTION: In the summer of 1966 'Battle of Britain' Class No 34088 *213 Squadron* negotiates Dorchester Junction on a Channel Islands boat train.**

   Dorchester Junction is now much more enclosed, but a glimpse of trains is still possible. On the last day of locomotive-hauled operation, 6 July 2002, the 17.15 service from Weymouth to Manchester Piccadilly was hauled by Class 47 No 47839. *Lawrence Golden/TG*

**DORCHESTER WEST (1): In the summer of 1965 the 1.05pm from Bristol Temple Meads to Weymouth passes Dorchester West behind a BR Standard Class 5.**

**On 6 July 2002 Class 150 No 150248 approaches Dorchester West forming the 17.22 all-stations service from Weymouth to Bristol Temple Meads. The embankment is completely overgrown, restricting the angle for the 'present' photograph.** *Lawrence Golden/TG*

**DORCHESTER WEST (2): '5700' Class No 5781 with two coaches forms the 9.28am Weymouth to Yeovil Pen Mill train on 10 January 1956.**

On 28 February 2004 Class 5MT No 73096 heads a return excursion to Victoria into Dorchester West. This train reversed at Yeovil Pen Mill for Yeovil Junction, then used the LSWR main line to London. *H. C. Casserley/TG*

**BRADFORD PEVERELL & STRATTON HALT is seen looking toward Dorchester in the early 1960s. The second view shows the halt in 2003; both platforms still exist, even though the halt closed in 1966 and the line was subsequently singled.** *Lens of Sutton/TG*

GRIMSTONE & FRAMPTON (1): On 29 August 1998 Class 37 No 37429 *Eisteddfod Genedlaethol*, in Regional Railways livery, works the 17.20 train from Weymouth to Bristol Temple Meads. This train was named the 'Weymouth Sand and Cycle Explorer' and is seen between Bradford Peverell & Stratton Halt and Grimstone & Frampton.

The first ever visit of a 'King' Class to the Weymouth-Yeovil line was recorded at the same location and is included because of its historic significance, although taken only a week after the upper photograph. The engine is No 6024 *King Edward I* and the train was named the 'Hardy Flyer'. *Both TG*

**GRIMSTONE & FRAMPTON (2):** 'Modified Hall' Class No 6983 *Otterington Hall* passes the station on a relief train from Wolverhampton on 17 July 1965.

The platforms have been removed, but the former goods yard is still in use, albeit as a road-only oil distribution depot. *Peter W. Gray/TG*

MAIDEN NEWTON (1): Two views taken 20 years apart – in the first DMU No B810 forms the 14.24 Weymouth to Bristol Temple Meads service on 15 June 1979, while on 9 July 1999 the 07.55 weedkilling train from Eastleigh to Exeter enters the station behind Class 37 No 37679, with sister engine No 37065 at the rear. *Both DHM*

MAIDEN NEWTON (2): The 8.40am from Weymouth has recently arrived at Maiden Newton on a wet day in January 1956. On the right is the stock for the Bridport branch.

The iron footbridge has been replaced by a concrete structure as Class 5MT No 73096 travels light from Yeovil Junction to Weymouth after bringing an excursion from Victoria on 28 February 2004. *H. C. Casserley/TG*

MAIDEN NEWTON (3): Single-car unit No W55032 arrives in the bay platform from the Bridport branch on 27 March 1967.

Today the bay is overgrown but still exists. On 19 July 2002 Class 31 31602 *Chimaera* pulls away from Maiden Newton on the 16.20 summer-Saturday-only train from Weymouth to Westbury. *Ronald Lumber/TG*

MAIDEN NEWTON (4): On 30 July 1980 a Weymouth to Bristol service is worked, as usual, by Class 118 DMUs. The leading unit is No P468.

The 'Hardy Flyer' (see page 26) stopped at Maiden Newton for a few minutes, enabling the photographer to get a second shot of this magnificent train as it departed for Yeovil on 5 September 1998. *Roger Marsh/TG*

EVERSHOT: Class 8F No 48431 enters Evershot station on a Bristol East Depot to Weymouth freight train on 14 August 1958, having been assisted up Evershot Bank.

Evershot station was closed in October 1966 and later demolished, but there is still plenty of evidence of its existence, including the approach road, gate-posts and railway cottages. On 5 August 1999 Class 37 No 37422 *Robert F. Fairlie Locomotive Engineer 1831-1885* passes the site of the station on the 14.33 Bristol Temple Meads to Weymouth train. *H. B. Priestley, courtesy Derek Phillips/TG*

**EVERSHOT BANK: Approaching Evershot Tunnel on 14 August 1960 is 'Castle' Class No 5099 *Compton Castle* on a Cardiff to Weymouth excursion. The train is being banked by Class 'U' No 31802.**

**A very special train ran from Perth to Maiden Newton on 2/3 October 2002. This was the Royal Train carrying Prince Charles, hauled by Class 47 No 47798 *Prince William*.** *S. C. Nash/TG*

CHETNOLE HALT, a little over 5 minutes walk from the village of the same name, is seen in July 1962. The halt is still open, but the original up wooden platform has been replaced by a concrete platform taken from Cattistock Halt between Evershot and Maiden Newton, the down platform having become redundant when the line was singled in 1968. On 25 July 2002 Wessex Trains ran a special train between Bristol and Weymouth for members of the Heart of Wessex Rail Partnership. This is the return working, being propelled at maximum line speed by Class 31 No 31459 *Cerberus*. The station is jocularly known as Chetnole Parkway. *C. L. Caddy/TG*

WINTERHAYS BRIDGE: First-generation DMUs of Classes 101 and 117 Nos C814 and B450 are seen at Winterhays Bridge between Chetnole and Yetminster forming the 15.05 Weymouth to Bristol Temple Meads service on 29 June 1985. The unit prefixes 'C' and 'B' indicate allocation to Cardiff and Bristol respectively.

Class 47 No 47783 *Saint Peter* works the 17.26 Weymouth to Bristol Temple Meads train on 30 July 1996 in lieu of the usual Class 37. *John Day/TG*

YETMINSTER station is seen at the beginning of the 20th century looking towards Yeovil. The station is in the village and still has a good service; it is referred to locally as Yetminster Central.

A track-recording train visits the line every few months. On 10 July 2003 this was top-and-tailed by Class 47 Nos 47778 *Irresistible* and 47732 *Restormel*. The old down platform still exists and is just visible in the undergrowth. *Classic Pictures/TG*

THORNFORD BRIDGE HALT (1) serves the villages of Thornford and Beer Hackett. To complete the trio of unofficial names of the request stops, this station is called Thornford International. Its layout is similar to Chetnole and it has met a similar fate, the remaining platform also coming from Cattistock Halt. The 'past' photograph shows the halt, looking towards Dorchester, in February 1967.

On 30 June 1995 the 19.38 service from Weymouth leaves Thornford on its way to Westbury behind Class 37 No 37412 *Driver John Elliot*. *C. L. Caddy/TG*

**THORNFORD BRIDGE HALT (2):** 'Modified Hall' Class No 7908 *Henshall Hall* passes the halt on a Birmingham to Weymouth Quay boat rain on 7 July 1962.

On 19 July 2003 Class 31 Nos 31468 *Hydra* and 31602 *Chimaera* take the 09.18 from Westbury towards Weymouth. For the 2004 summer season the stock was painted in Wessex Trains livery. *C. L. Caddy/TG*

CLIFTON MAYBANK (1): The Clifton Maybank area is marked by attractive scenery with the railway passing through a deep but wide cutting. 'Hall' Class No 5963 *Wimpole Hall* hauls a Weymouth to Wolverhampton train on 25 August 1962.

Double-heading was very unusual on locomotive-hauled trains in the 1990s, but on 7 July 1997 the 17.26 Weymouth to Bristol Temple Meads train was worked by Class 37 Nos 37427 and 37412 *Driver John Elliot*. *John Day/TG*

**CLIFTON MAYBANK (2): Class 5MT No 73080 passes with an up freight train on 8 August 1965. Although the view is partially blocked today, the location is still worth a visit. On 19 July 2002 a train on a crew training run, with Class 31s Nos 31190** *Gryphon* **and 31459** *Cerberus*, **makes its way to Weymouth.** *John Day/TG*

CLIFTON MAYBANK (3): Class 3 Hymek No D7093 is seen at Clifton Maybank on a Bank Holiday special to Weymouth in April 1966. In the foreground is the LSWR main line from Waterloo to Yeovil Junction and Exeter Central.

The line on the extreme left from Yeovil Junction to Pen Mill is now hidden from view by trees; although it is still in use, there is no regular passenger service. On 2 August 1999 Class 37 No 37424 takes the 09.00 from Bristol Temple Meads to Weymouth. *Ronald Lumber/TG*

CLIFTON MAYBANK (4): 'Hall' Class No 4909 *Blakesley Hall* works an up special on 24 June 1961 between Clifton Maybank and Yeovil South Junction, which is situated just before Pen Mill station. On the right is the line connecting Yeovil Town and Pen Mill with Yeovil Junction.

On 21 August 2002 Class 31s Nos 31459 *Cerberus* and 31190 *Gryphon* work a special train to Weymouth. The bridge over a stream is just visible in the extreme right of both photographs. *John Day/TG*

# Abbotsbury branch

**UPWEY:** This was the view looking towards Bridport from Upwey in the early 1950s prior to closure, which came in 1952. Freight services were retained between Upwey Junction (Upwey & Broadwey) and Upwey until January 1962, but the freight service beyond Upwey was withdrawn at the same time as passenger services. The station building is now used for other purposes and the yard by a coal merchant. At the other end of the station is a builders' merchant. *Lens of Sutton/TG*

**ABBOTSBURY** was the terminus of the branch, seen here looking towards Upwey in 1910. The area used by the station is now occupied by bungalows, although remnants of the platform can still be found. *Lens of Sutton/TG*

# West Bay branch

**TOLLER is seen here from the cab of an approaching DMU on 10 August 1960. Although the area is very overgrown today, the platform can still be seen from the adjacent public footpath.**
*Derek Phillips/TG*

46

**BRIDPORT: In the first view the 3.35pm train to Maiden Newton waits to leave Bridport on 8 September 1953 behind '4500' Class No 4562.**

**On 26 April 1975, just before final closure of the branch, Class 121 single-coach unit No B135 leaves Bridport for Maiden Newton.**

**Since closure the site has been redeveloped, and as best can be judged this is the equivalent view, as seen in August 2002. Alignment with the 'past' views was by reference to old buildings in the background and the adjacent minor roads.** *T. G. Wassell, courtesy Hugh Davies/Barry Thirlwall/TG*

**EAST STREET: This is the level crossing at East Street, with the station immediately to the right, in the early 1900s. All trace of the station has gone, and a roundabout occupies part of the site. The location is identified by the house on the left immediately beyond the level crossing in the 'past' photograph.** *Classic Pictures/TG*

**WEST BAY:** The terminus is seen from the buffer stops at the turn of the 20th century. Despite losing its passenger service in 1930, the station survives and has been pleasantly restored; the only obvious change to the building is the cutting back of the canopy. It was used for a short period in the late 1990s as a tourist office, but closed in 2001. A 'Portakabin' occupies the position held only a few years ago by two coaches in use as offices. *Classic Pictures/TG*

# Lyme Regis

**LYME REGIS: The Adams radial tank engines of Class 0415 were synonymous with the Lyme Regis branch, where they worked for decades. Class 0415 No 30584 heads the 4.42pm from Axminster at Lyme Regis on 13 August 1960.**

**Light industrial units now occupy the station site. Part of the line is a public footpath, but significant sections of the trackbed are in private ownership. Apart from the Lyme Regis area, the line is in Devon.** *Both TG*

# Weymouth Quay

WEYMOUTH TRAMWAY (1): On 3 July 1966 ex-LMSR 2MT tank engine No 41298 edges a rake of SR Bulleid coaches along the quayside toward the terminus.

On 2 May 1999 a special train ran from Yeovil Junction to Weymouth Quay, and is seen here on the quayside behind Class 73 electro-diesel No 73138. The tramway, although officially still open, has not been used for several years. *Lawrence Golden/TG*

**WEYMOUTH TRAMWAY (2):** A boat train from Waterloo conveying Channel Island passengers runs along the quayside in 1961 hauled by '5700' Class No 3759.

A special train inappropriately called the 'Ocean Liner Express', ran from Waterloo on 18 December 1994, and is seen here on the quayside hauled by Class 33 No 33116 *Hertfordshire Rail Tours. DHM collection/TG*

London and South Western
RAILWAY. (787D.)

*From*

To

# JERSEY

[W. & S. Ltd.]

53

**WEYMOUTH QUAY:** The first photograph shows steam and diesel at Weymouth Quay in October 1962. On the left is Class 03 No D2397 and in the platform is '5700' Class No 3737 on a boat train.

By 18 September 1970 steam had long been banished, but No 2397 is still operating, on a train of conflats, with sister engine No 2180 on a boat train.

On 18 December 1994 Class 33 No 33116 *Hertfordshire Rail Tours* works the return 'Ocean liner Express'. *DHM collection/ Barry Thirlwall/TG*

# Weymouth to Portland

MELCOMBE REGIS: The line from Weymouth to Portland and Easton closed to passengers on 3 March 1952, but was kept open for several more years for the occasional special train. One such train has just arrived at Melcombe Regis from Easton on 8 July 1956, hauled by '5700' Class No 4621.

The same location in April 1995 shows that the site had become a car park, and a later visit in 2003 found that buildings have now been erected. *Hugh Davies/TG*

WESTHAM BRIDGE is seen here on 22 November 1970. In the background the roof of the goods shed at Weymouth is visible, beyond which is Weymouth station.

The present-day view, taken on 3 October 2002, shows that the bridge has been completely removed and the landscape has changed. The few surviving buildings identify the location. *Barry Thirlwall/TG*

**RODWELL: This early photograph of Rodwell is looking towards Portland and was taken from the adjacent road bridge. The view from that bridge is now blocked by trees, so a lower elevation was used to show the scene on 24 November 2002. The trackbed has become a public footpath.** *Lens of Sutton/TG*

**SANDSFOOT CASTLE HALT** was not opened until 1932 and was therefore used for only 20 years. It was familiar to one of the authors (TG) from childhood days on holiday from home in Surrey, and the remains are seen here on 19 April 1970, looking north. Even in 2002 part of the wooden platform still survives. *Barry Thirlwall/TG*

WYKE REGIS HALT was also photographed on 19 April 1970. The rusting footbridge was hardly warranted, even in the heyday of the branch, as trains were not very frequent, did not travel at great speed, and almost all stopped at the halt. A torpedo factory was situated just to the left of the halt; it closed in 1994 and was demolished three years later, to be replaced by houses. Virtually nothing remains of the halt today and the trackbed is a cycle and footpath. *Barry Thirlwall/TG*

G. W. & Southern Rys.

Portland             Portland

987    TO    8.7

WYKE REGIS HALT

THIRD CLASS

4½d. C    Fare    4½d. C

Wyke Regis          Wyke Regis

FOR CONDITIONS SEE BACK (W.L

987

**EASTON:** The terminus at Easton occupied a cramped site, as can be seen in this 1950s photograph of a Class 'O2' and a rake of LSWR coaches.

The view today is particularly uninspiring, although slightly more informative in winter when leaves are not completely obliterating the view. *Lens of Sutton/TG*

**1189**

SOUTHERN & G.W.RYS
Issued subject to the Byelaws
Regulations & Conditions in the
Companies Bills and Notices.

RAIL MOTOR CAR

MONTHLY
as advertised

Third Class
Fare 1/8

(C)
BETWEEN

Melcombe Regis
&
EASTON
and RETURN

NOT
Transferable.

The Passenger is requested
to see this ticket punched at
the time of issue

JAN FEB MAR APR MAY JUN  JUL AUG SEP OCT NOV DEC

# Dorchester South to Wareham

**DORCHESTER SOUTH (1):** The first photograph shows the view from the end of the up terminal platform at Dorchester in June 1966, with the down through platform on the right.

A further visit to Dorchester was made on 15 August 1986 when the old up-side terminus was being demolished and facilities for the relatively new up through platform were being built.

The third photograph shows the present-day scene, with the old platform behind the retaining wall. On the right, part of the roof of an up train is just visible. *Bernard Mills/TG (2)*

DORCHESTER SOUTH (2): In the foreground is the down platform, and the train on the up through line is the 10.15am from Weymouth on 3 June 1966, hauled by Standard 4MT No 76005; it will reverse into the up platform before proceeding all-stations to Bournemouth Central.

On 25 March 2004 newly delivered 'Desiro' unit No 450017 is under test between Weymouth and Bournemouth. Once commissioned, these units will replace the BR Mark I EMUs currently used on outer suburban lines. *Both TG*

DORCHESTER SOUTH (3): This is the station just after rebuilding had been completed, with conventional up and down platforms; the up spur was on the left, starting approximately where the rear of the train is positioned. There used to be an engine shed on the right and a signal box just beyond the new houses. The train is the 16.31 Weymouth to Waterloo consisting of Class 33 No 33111 and Class 438 (4-TC) No 8022.

The lines through the platforms are now signalled for reversible working, beyond which it is single line as far as Moreton. A train of empty hopper wagons runs from Eastleigh to Wool once a week, and to avoid causing congestion at Wool level crossing it runs on to Dorchester South for the locomotive to run round. On 24 June 2002 Class 66 No 66239 is in the process of running round its train prior to returning to Wool. *Both TG*

**MORETON (I):** In June 1967, during the final days of steam, a BR Standard 76xxx 4MT, carrying no numberplate, enters the station on a Weymouth train. Passing the same point on 27 May 1987 is Class 33 No 33111 with Class 438 (4-TC) unit No 8020 forming the 07.16 service from Bournemouth to Weymouth.

*Bernard Mills/TG*

MORETON (2): This general view of the station was taken in 1964, looking towards Bournemouth. The station has since been rebuilt with only basic shelters. On 30 July 2001 a Class 442 EMU leaves with the 14.48 service from Weymouth to Waterloo. *C. L. Caddy/TG*

WOOL station, well endowed with staff, is seen in LSWR days, looking towards Weymouth. Although the buildings lasted well into BR days, they have now been replaced with the usual featureless boxes. After laying derelict for decades, the sidings were re-instated for the outward transport of sand and a weekly service introduced. On 13 August 2001 Class 66 No 66202 enters the station with the empties. *Classic Pictures/TG*

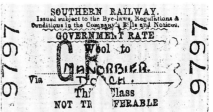

WORGRET JUNCTION is located about 1¼ miles west of Wareham and is where the Swanage branch diverges from the main line. On 11 April 1964 Class 'M7' 0-4-4T No 30053 is crossing to the up line with the 11.40am Swanage to Wareham service. The junction and signal box are just out of view to the left.

After closure of the line to Swanage in January 1972, the first 3 miles of the branch were retained to serve the sidings at Furzebrook. The signal box closed in 1976 and the junction is now controlled from a ground frame. The crossover was taken out of use at the same time and trains from the branch now run 'wrong line' to Wareham. In September 2002 half a mile of mothballed track between Norden (the present limit of the Swanage Railway) and Furzebrook was re-instated and special dispensation was granted for a Virgin Trains Class 220 to run from the national network to Swanage. However, the current arrangement at Worgret is unsuited to regular passenger traffic and is one of the obstacles to be overcome before the Swanage Railway achieves its aim of running into Wareham. The present-day view shows the 14.48 Weymouth-Waterloo service passing the junction on 24 February 2003. *TG/DHM*

WAREHAM (1): An express from Waterloo approaches Wareham on 27 May 1987. The unidentified Class 33 is in charge of two Class 438 (4-TC) units; these had left Waterloo at 06.44 propelled by a 4-REP EMU, which had been detached at Bournemouth.

On 6 July 2002 Class 47 No 47839 works the Saturdays-only Virgin Trains 09.10 Liverpool to Weymouth train. *Both TG*

**WAREHAM (2): In the station, Class 4MT No 76008 is working a Bournemouth to Weymouth local train in October 1966. A connecting DMU for Swanage can be seen in the bay platform.**

**In the spring of 1987 push-pull-operated Class 33 No 33115 hauls Class 438 (4-TC) unit No 8026 forming the 06.44 Waterloo to Weymouth service.**

**The modern image is represented on 6 July 2002 by Class 442 EMU No 2412 forming the 13.00 service from Waterloo, which terminated at Wareham.** *Bernard Mills/TG (2)*

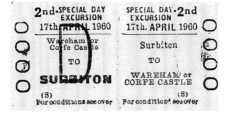

# Swanage line

CORFE VIADUCT: Ivatt 2-6-2T No 41316 is pictured from East Hill on 7 August 1965 as it passes over the four-arched Purbeck stone viaduct on the approach to Corfe Castle station with a train bound for Swanage. The Norman castle is built on a natural mound, the lower levels of which are just visible on the left. In the middle distance the railway passes under a bridge that carried Fayle's Tramway from china clay mines to Norden (formerly Eldon) siding, where the tramway connected with the branch. The transfer shed can just be seen beyond the second overbridge.

The siding was taken out of use in 1966 and the viaduct is becoming obscured by trees. The Swanage Railway established a park-and-ride station at Norden in 1995 and Standard 2-6-4Ts Nos 80078 and 80104 are working the 11.30 departure from there on 15 September 2002. *Peter W. Gray/DHM*

CORFE CASTLE: In April 1963 Class 'M7' No 30667 is about to depart by propelling its Swanage to Wareham push-pull train. Just visible in the small goods yard to the left is one of two Pullman cars being used as camping coaches. Part of the ruined castle can be glimpsed on the hill in the right background. Both of the original branch stations – here and Swanage – have buildings constructed of attractive Purbeck stone.

All the sidings here were taken out of use in 1965, but the passing loop remained until closure of the branch. This loop has now been re-instated, and stabled in the down platform, not currently used for passengers, is a Class 108 DMU (Nos 51933 and 54504) in September 2002. *Lawrence Golden/DHM*

SWANAGE (1): The single-road engine shed, a sub-shed to Bournemouth, was also built of local stone. A 50-foot turntable was sited immediately outside, and this had to be operated before locomotives could enter the building due to the track orientation in this cramped location. On 12 June 1964 Standard 4MT 2-6-4T No 80146 passes with the 9.50am train from Wareham. Until 1958 the shed possessed an arched entrance, but this was altered after an 'M7' tank overshot the turntable and collided with the building!

The shed closed in 1966, and although the turntable was removed, luckily the building survived into the preservation era. On 15 September 2002 'Merchant Navy' Class No 35027 *Port Line* is being coaled, as 'S15' 4-6-0 No 828 passes with the 13.00 service from Norden. *John Scrace/DHM*

SWANAGE (2): Standard 3MT 2-6-2T No 82029 passes the goods shed as it approaches the main platform at the terminus on 11 April 1964 with the 3.37pm train from Wareham. The starting signal for the bay platform is visible, with the signal box just out of view to the left. The flat-roofed hut was constructed as an air-raid shelter during the Second World War.

The goods shed is another survivor, but today most of the yard is used as a bus and car park. Bullied 'Pacific' *Port Line* can just be seen in September 2002. *TG/DHM*

SWANAGE (3): The view from the buffer stops on 12 October 1971 is a depressing one as 'Berkshire' DMU No 1127 awaits its 13.40 departure to Wareham. The branch had been completely dieselised in September 1966 with all track at Swanage, other than a single running line, taken out of use in the following June. Closure came less than three months later on New Year's Day 1972.

Thirty years on there is a far happier scene with re-instated track, a busy platform and locomotives Nos 34072 *257 Squadron* and D3591 all providing evidence of a thriving railway. *Ronald Lumber/DHM*

# Wareham to Christchurch

HOLTON HEATH station opened in April 1916 adjacent to a Naval cordite works. Originally used by workers at this factory, it was made available to the public in 1924. An extensive railway network served the works, but this closed with the factory in 1961. Two reception roads survived until 1968, and the remains of the crossover leading to these are visible on 15 June 1979, as Class 33 33106, with 4-TC units Nos 401 and 432, approaches forming the 15.35 Waterloo to Weymouth service.

The station now serves an industrial estate that has been built on the site of the works. No trains call on Sundays. The 13.30 Waterloo-Weymouth service approaches at speed on 15 September 2002. *Both DHM*

HAMWORTHY JUNCTION was originally known as Poole Junction when the Southampton & Dorchester Railway opened in 1847, a branch from here leading to Poole's first station in Lower Hamworthy. The name was changed in 1872 when the Broadstone to Poole branch opened, with passengers now changing at the former location. The west end of the station is depicted on 16 March 1963 with Standard 4MT 2-6-0 No 76012 standing at the Hamworthy branch platform; the branch runs off to the right.

The signal box still survives on the other end of the down platform and controls both the main line and access to the branch. The surviving semaphore signal is, however, non-operational and is used to halt branch trains for the collection of the single-line token. *C. L. Caddy/DHM*

**HAMWORTHY GOODS: The passenger station here lasted until 1896, but the branch has survived into the 21st century as a freight-only line, and has hosted a number of passenger specials over the years. One such occasion was 16 October 1966, when Standard 3MT 2-6-0 No 77014 worked the 'Dorset & Hants Railtour'.**

Current freight services use the site of the old cement terminal adjacent to Hamworthy Junction. A scrap train is loaded there each week, and the site is also used as an aggregate distribution depot. On 29 May 1998 Class 37 No 37798 has taken its train down the branch after unloading, and has run round before departing for Merehead Quarry in the Mendips. *John Scrace/DHM*

POOLE (1): On 8 July 1971 Hymek diesel-hydraulic No D7036 brings the empty stock for the 16.29 departure to Birmingham from the carriage sidings into the station. The siding on the left leads to the down bay platform, which was used for parcels and goods traffic, although until 1960 this use was limited as the track also provided access to the Poole Quay tramway. Visible in the distance is the 'B' signal box, which was named Poole West until 1949, and to the right is the sizeable goods yard that had been extended in 1941.

The siding and most of the track in the goods yard has now been lifted. However, the signal box survives, and the platforms have been lengthened to serve the electrified railway. 'Wessex Electric' No 2407 forms the 16.40 Weymouth-Waterloo service on 22 September 2002. *John Scrace/DHM*

POOLE (2): The immediate approach to the station from the east is made via a 10-chain curve that at one time also included two level crossings. On 17 June 1967 Standard 5MT 4-6-0 No 73093 passes over the second of these (Towngate Street) while working the 7.50am Bournemouth to Weymouth stopper.

This crossing was replaced by a flyover in 1971, and this dominates the September 2002 scene as Class 442 EMU No 2412 arrives with the 15.30 Waterloo to Weymouth service. *Tony Wardle/DHM*

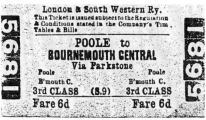

London & South Western Ry.
This Ticket is issued subject to the Regulation
& Conditions stated in the Company's Tim
Tables & Bills

**POOLE to**
**BOURNEMOUTH CENTRAL**
**Via Parkstone**

Poole               Poole
B'mouth C.        B'mouth C.
**3rd CLASS**   (S.9)   **3rd CLASS**
**Fare 6d**          **Fare 6d**

POOLE QUAY: A street tramway opened on 15 June 1874 to connect Poole station with the busy Town Quay. This goods-only branch was extended in 1893 when the quay itself was extended, giving a total route length of just over a mile. The line was single with two passing loops until it reached Custom House, where the greater width of the quay allowed two tracks. On 15 July 1959 Class 'B4' 0-4-0T No 30093 is standing just before the commencement of this section. Originally horses were used on the line, but steam locomotives were introduced in about 1899. The 'B4s' arrived in 1904 and lasted until closure of the line.

With many ships using Hamworthy rather than Poole Quay, and also with the greater use of road transport, traffic declined to such an extent that the line was closed in 1960; the final train running on 30 April. The present-day scene was recorded on a wet 1 December 2003. *DHM collection/DHM*

PARKSTONE: The station nameboard reads 'Parkstone for Sandbanks', referring to Poole's beaches, 3 miles to the south. A 2-mile-long incline at 1 in 60, known as Parkstone Bank, commences about a mile east of Poole station, but eases to 1 in 300 through this location. Viewed from the station footbridge, and to be withdrawn the following month, 'West Country' Class 'Pacific' No 34101 *Hartland* has assistance from a banking engine as it heads a Weymouth to Waterloo express in June 1966. The goods yard to the left had been taken out of use the previous October. A tramway had run south from this yard to serve a pottery.

Housing now stands on the site of the yard, but the station is still open. Class 421 (4-CIG) EMUs Nos 1887 and 1882 approach forming the 14.06 Poole to Waterloo service on 21 February 2003. *Bernard Mills/DHM*

BRANKSOME (1): The station is located in a shallow cutting, and its brick buildings are on two levels, the booking hall and parcels office at street level, with a covered footbridge leading directly from this building to the down platform. This can be observed on the right of this 12 April 1963 view, with the signal box just visible in the left distance.

The building still stands, although modified, and the booking office is still manned. The signal box continued in use until December 2003, but has since been closed under the Dorset Coast re-signalling scheme. *C. L. Caddy/DHM*

BRANKSOME (2): A junction is located immediately to the east of the station, with one line running to the left to Bournemouth Central and the other to the right, originally serving Branksome engine shed, carriage sidings and terminating at Bournemouth West. A further chord connected these two routes and completed a triangular junction. This east chord closed in November 1965 when the area was being re-modelled prior to electrification; it was then no longer possible for stock to move directly from the carriage sidings to Bournemouth Central without reversing in Branksome station. In this scene from June 1966 a Standard 4MT 2-6-0 has brought such a working to a stand with 'West Country' Class No 34006 *Bude* at the rear. The Bullied 'Pacific' is now ready to take the stock forward to Bournemouth Central.

Class 442 No 2421 departs forming the 10.40 Weymouth to Waterloo service on 23 February 2003. *Bernard Mills/DHM*

BOURNEMOUTH WEST JUNCTION: Class 5MT No 73019 with the 12.43pm from Poole descends the 1 in 90 into Bournemouth West on 10 September 1959. Bournemouth West lost more and more of its trains with the closure of the Salisbury line, the Ringwood loop and the SDJR, all within the space of two years.

Bournemouth West closed in October 1965, but Bournemouth Depot is still open and used for the servicing and berthing of EMUs. On the occasion of an open day at the depot on 15 May 1998, a shuttle service was run from Bournemouth (Central) using Class 159 DMU No 159017. Note the platelayers' hut in both photographs. *Both TG*

**CARRIAGE SIDINGS: Class 'M7' No 30112 heads the 12.26pm Bournemouth West to Brockenhurst train, which ran via Ringwood, on 10 September 1959.**

**Following withdrawal, the Eastleigh-built motor luggage vans of Class 931 were stored at Bournemouth Depot pending disposal. This is No 091, formerly 9001, on 27 August 1997. The vehicle is now at Shepherdswell on the East Kent Railway.** *Both TG*

BOURNEMOUTH WEST (1): Bournemouth was ignored during the early years of railway development in Dorset due to being only a small coastal village, and it was not until 1874 that the LSWR's branch from Poole was extended to reach western Bournemouth. Originally this station had two platforms but was expanded over the years as services developed. On 6 June 1963 Standard 4MT 2-6-4T No 80083 has arrived with a portion of the 10.30am from Waterloo, and is now backing the stock from Platform 5 up the incline towards the carriage sidings.

Following demolition of the terminus, the Wessex Way bypass was constructed through the site. *Derek Frost/DHM*

BOURNEMOUTH WEST (2): The station had six platforms in its final form, and Standard 4MT 2-6-0 No 76027 is standing at No 3 on 6 June 1963 with the 6.48pm departure to Templecombe. This view illustrates the supporting struts that linked the two platform canopies on the northern side of the station. The steel canopy for Platforms 1 and 2 on the right was a later addition.

That canopy hid the Midland Hotel, which is located outside the station, but it is clearly visible in February 2003, with a car park in the foreground and the Wessex Way just out of sight to the left. *Derek Frost/DHM*

(8/50) 24M

SOUTHERN
BRITISH RAILWAYS
REGION

Stock
787

TO

# BOURNEMOUTH WEST

**BOURNEMOUTH SHED:** When Central station opened a locomotive depot was established on a cramped site just to the west of the station. Subsequently a second building was added and other facilities were improved over the years. In 1936 the shed was extended with extra pits provided. At this time the 50-foot turntable was replaced by a new 65-foot example, and on 19 September 1952 'Lord Nelson' Class 4-6-0 No 30862 *Lord Collingwood* stands next to it.

The depot closed with the end of steam operations on the Southern Region in 1967, and the site was cleared soon afterward to make way for a car park. The Wessex Way flyover now crosses the former shed yard at this spot. *Derek Frost/DHM*

BOURNEMOUTH CENTRAL (1): Stabled at Bournemouth Central on 16 May 1987 are EMU Class 432 (4-REP) No 2007 and electro-diesel Class 73 No 73114. At the same location on 5 July 2002 is Virgin HST power car No 43100 sandwiched between two Class 442 EMUs. *Both TG*

BOURNEMOUTH CENTRAL (2): Class 73 No 73114 enters the station on the 16.00 train to Waterloo with Class 492 (5-TCB) 2801 and Class 438 (4-TC) No 8031 on 16 May 1987. Both these classes were introduced on a temporary basis during the transition from 4-REP units to the new Class 442 'Wessex Electrics', which used motors from the former vehicles.

On 5 July 2002 the Hamworthy to Cardiff Tidal scrap metal train was worked by Class 60 No 60037. *Both TG*

BOURNEMOUTH CENTRAL (3): The splendid train shed provides a backdrop to Class 'T9' 4-4-0 No 30119 on 19 September 1952. The engine had earlier worked up from Weymouth and, after turning, is standing on the down through road before working the 7.12pm departure back to Weymouth.

The through roads were removed prior to electrification, but the station has recently undergone extensive renovation. On 21 February 2003 Virgin Trains 'Voyager' No 220013 has arrived forming the 08.44 service from Newcastle. *Derek Frost/DHM*

BOURNEMOUTH CENTRAL (4): Two Class 33s, Nos 33113 and 33105, have been attached at Bournemouth to work the 13.32 from Waterloo to Weymouth on 16 May 1987. The leading unit is Class 438 (4-TC) No 8012. Fifteen years later, on 5 July 2002, up and down Class 442 'Wessex Electrics' pass at Bournemouth. *Both TG*

BOURNEMOUTH CENTRAL (5): 'West Country' Class No 34097 *Holsworthy* leaves Bournemouth Central with the 5.40pm service to Eastleigh on 6 June 1963. The train is about to enter the 50-yard-long Holdenhurst Road Tunnel, which could be more accurately described as a bridge. Beyond this is a goods yard that occupies the site of the original Bournemouth East station. This closed in 1885 when Central opened, although initially the new facility had the suffix 'East'.

The goods yard closed to rail traffic in June 1979. Class 412 (4-CEP) EMU No 2316 departs forming the 15.06 Poole to Waterloo service on 21 February 2003. *Derek Frost/DHM*

POKESDOWN (1): This station originally had a single island platform with a signal box positioned on its west end. In 1930/31 the station was rebuilt with four tracks and two outer platforms, the quadrupling providing a passing facility, and a new unusual signal box of steel construction was provided at the west end of the up platform. This can be seen on All Fools Day 1967 as 'West Country' Class 'Pacific' No 34098 *Templecombe* storms past with the 4.37pm Bournemouth to Waterloo 'Bournemouth Belle' Pullman train.

The signal box closed in December 1972. Class 58 No 58015 approaches with the 17.27 Hamworthy to Merehead Quarry stone empties on a wet 31 July 1998. *Tony Wardle/DHM*

POKESDOWN (2): The station was named Boscombe when it opened in 1886, but was renamed Pokesdown (Boscombe) five years later, then the suffix was dropped when Boscombe station opened less than a mile to the west in 1897. Standard 5MT 4-6-0 No 73085 speeds through with the 11.30am Waterloo to Bournemouth express in August 1966.

The down through line was taken out of use in September 1971, and the up centre road lasted until December 1972 when the west end of the up platform was demolished. The station still serves its local population and on 24 February 2003 Class 421 (4-CIG) No 1306 departs with the 07.45 Waterloo to Poole service. *Lawrence Golden/DHM*

CHRISTCHURCH (1): The railway reached here in 1862 in the form of a branch from Ringwood, but the original station was replaced in 1886 by a new facility a short distance to the west in readiness for the arrival of the direct double-track main line from Brockenhurst, which opened in March 1888. Class 'U' 2-6-0 No 31790 pauses with the 5.05pm Southampton Terminus to Bournemouth train in July 1965.

The footbridge has lost its roof but otherwise the 24 February 2003 scene does not look too different, as Class 442 No 2415 calls with the 10.30 Waterloo to Weymouth service. *Lawrence Golden/DHM*

CHRISTCHURCH (2): Unrebuilt 'West Country' Class No 34041 *Wilton* passes with the Manchester to Bournemouth 'Pines Express' on 28 July 1964. This celebrated train had run via the Somerset & Dorset line until September 1962 and thereafter via Basingstoke. The tall signal box was designed to allow the signalman a clear view over the adjacent road bridge. The track on the left leads to the goods yard and the route of the branch to Ringwood; the original station had been located on this curve.

The signal box closed in December 1972, with the goods yard taken out of use one month later. Class 421 (4-CIG) No 1884 forms the 09.45 Waterloo to Poole service in February 2003. *DHM collection/DHM*

# Lines from Broadstone Junction

BROADSTONE JUNCTION (1): This location saw its first trains in 1847 when the Southampton & Dorchester Railway opened. A station was opened as New Poole Junction in 1872 to serve the new branch line to Poole, then in 1885 the Somerset & Dorset arrived via a spur from Corfe Mullen Junction. The station was renamed five times in its lifetime, eventually being simply branded as Broadstone in July 1929. 'West Country' Class No 34092 *City of Wells* departs from one of its four platforms with the 6.20pm Weymouth to Salisbury train on 30 August 1961.

Since closure the Broadstone Leisure Centre has been erected on the site of the station. *TG/DHM*

BROADSTONE JUNCTION (2): Also on 30 August 1961 Class 2P 4-4-0 No 40634 is seen at the north end of the station while working the 5.30pm Bournemouth West to Templecombe. Built in 1928 for the Somerset & Dorset, it will take the single-track SDJR line to Corfe Mullen, which can just be seen running off to the left. The original line from Wimborne runs straight ahead.

Instead of a timeless railway scene, the September 2002 image is of tennis courts and housing. Is this progress? *TG/DHM*

BAILEY GATE station opened when the Dorset Central Railway commenced operations from Wimborne to Blandford in 1860. It was initially named after the adjacent village of Sturminster Marshall until Sturminster Newton station opened. To avoid any confusion it was then renamed after a gate on the nearby turnpike road. Sidings were added in 1919 to serve a dairy that produced much traffic for the railway. On 23 October 1965 Standard 3MT 2-6-2T No 82041 stands 'wrong line' with the afternoon milk train to Templecombe. The engine had earlier worked the 8.15am local from Bath to Templecombe.

Since closure the whole site, including the former dairy, has been redeveloped as an industrial estate, with new units also erected. An entrance gatehouse has been built where the up platform once stood. *Hugh Ballantyne/DHM*

SPETISBURY: The line from Bailey Gate to Blandford was single track when opened, and this was another of the original stations. This section was doubled in April 1901 when a second platform and signal box were provided. This undated view from the original, and now down, platform shows these 'new' facilities and is possibly a contemporary record of these developments.

The station was later downgraded to a halt and finally closed in September 1956, the signal box having closed in 1952. Both platforms still survive, although they are becoming overgrown, and the trackbed is used as a footpath. *Classic Pictures/DHM*

BLANDFORD FORUM: This important market town appears to have had the suffix added to its name in the 19th century, but the railway did not follow suit until 1953. The line from here to Templecombe remained single track and in this undated scene an up train is waiting to cross a southbound working. The down train is passing under a metal footbridge provided for the general public, the station having a subway for passengers.

The line south of here remained open for goods traffic until January 1969, but since closure houses have been erected over much of the site. However, the footbridge survives with a path following the trackbed to the northern outskirts of the town. The present view allows a closer view of the bridge and a short section of track that provides a memorial to the railway. *Classic Pictures/DHM*

SHILLINGSTONE: Standard 5MT 4-6-0 No 73054 departs with the 1.10pm from Bournemouth in July 1965. The 16-lever signal box can be noted, with the goods yard, containing two concrete-built stores, to the left of the engine; goods traffic had ceased three months earlier.

The goods yard has been developed as a small industrial estate, but the two stores remain and their roofs are visible above those of new units in September 2002. The main station building and platforms also survive, but are obscured by trees. The North Dorset Railway Trust has launched a project to renovate the building to include a museum, repair the platforms and fencing, rebuild the signal box and other buildings, and relay a stretch of track. *Lawrence Golden/DHM*

STURMINSTER NEWTON: Passenger services over the Somerset & Dorset should have ceased on 3 January 1966, but due to problems in organising replacement bus services, a limited timetable of four trains each way was provided until closure was finally effected from 7 March that year. Recorded during this temporary reprieve, Standard 4MT No 80013 is working the 9.37am Bournemouth Central to Templecombe train on 26 February.

Much of the station area is now a car park. The goods shed just visible in the 'past' view has been demolished, but other buildings from the railway era survive to the left and helped to align the 2002 picture. A footpath follows the trackbed south of here. *Hugh Ballantyne/DHM*

STALBRIDGE: Two BR Standard engines meet on 15 October 1965: 4MT 2-6-4T No 80134 waits with the 4.13pm Evercreech Junction to Bournemouth Central train, while the signalman is about to exchange tokens with the crew of approaching 5MT 4-6-0 No 73001 with the 3.40pm Bournemouth to Bristol service. The 18-lever signal box controlled a level crossing in addition to the passing loop and a small goods yard, and remained in use until the line closed.

Today a bump in Station Road marks the site of the crossing. To the right of this, rails in the road are remnants of a siding that once extended across it. Otherwise there is no trace of the railway, with a large industrial unit and associated car park covering the site of the station. *Ronald Lumber/DHM*

WIMBORNE: The station opened in June 1847 when the Southampton & Dorchester Railway commenced operations. When the Dorset Central branch to Blandford opened, it was initially operated by the LSWR, but was to become part of the Somerset & Dorset after only three years. This station was built on a curve and in the first view, from the north on 30 August 1961, the 7.08pm Bournemouth West to Brockenhurst is depicted. This push-pull train, consisting of Set 662, was being propelled by Class 'M7' tank No 30050.

Passenger services over this line ended in May 1964, but freight facilities were provided here until 1977. The second view, from a little further to the north in June 1970, shows the tall 29-lever signal box, which had closed in January 1967. Also visible is a Class 33 diesel locomotive on a demolition train.

Today an industrial estate covers the site of the station. *TG(2)/DHM*

WEST MOORS was a junction station, and opened in August 1867, almost eight months after the Salisbury & Dorset had connected with the Southampton & Dorchester. In a busy scene from 30 August 1961, Class 'U' 2-6-0 No 31637 waits to leave with the 1.03pm Bournemouth West to Salisbury train, while Standard 4MT No 76059 approaches with the 12.50pm Salisbury-Bournemouth West service. The centre signal on the gantry controls access to a War Department petrol depot that had opened in 1943.

Passenger services ceased in 1964, but traffic to this depot continued until 1974. All trace of the railway has now gone, and the February 2003 view shows that accommodation for the elderly now stands on this site. *TG/DHM*

ASHLEY HEATH HALT: Located about a mile from the Hampshire boundary, this halt was opened on the west side of Woolsbridge Crossing in April 1927. The level crossing was controlled from a small signal box, which is behind the camera in this picture, taken three weeks prior to closure on 4 May 1964.

The route of the railway here now forms part of the Castleman Trailpath, named after the Wimborne solicitor who promoted the building of the line. The west end of the up platform has been restored but is not visible from the site of the crossing. *TG/DHM*

# Yeovil Junction to Gillingham

**YEOVIL JUNCTION (1): This station was in Dorset, but is now in Somerset following boundary changes in 1995. The authors have nevertheless included some present-day, as well as 'past' photographs. Here an up freight train behind Class 'N' No 31792 approaches Yeovil Junction on 13 August 1964.**

**On 6 July 2003 'Deltic' Class 55 No D9016 (55016)** *Gordon Highlander* **worked a special from Exeter to Waterloo as far as Yeovil Junction. The signal box at this end of the station has been demolished but the one at the London end is still in use.** *Both TG*

YEOVIL JUNCTION (2): Type 4 'Warship' No D832 *Onslaught* heads the 9.00am Waterloo to Exeter train at Yeovil Junction on 2 July 1967. These engines were displaced by Class 33s, then 50s, then briefly by Class 47s and more recently by Class 159 DMUs. On the extreme left is the Junction to Town shuttle train.

On 28 June 2003 a Class 47, No 47733 *Eastern Star*, returned to Yeovil on an evening circular excursion from Bristol via Westbury and back via Exeter and Taunton. The platform buildings on the extreme right no longer have a canopy and there is no access via the footbridge. The buildings are in use by Network Rail and the South West Main Line Steam Company. The old coal yard, on the left beyond the photograph, is occupied by the Somerset and Dorset Locomotive Company Ltd. *Ronald Lumber/TG*

**YEOVIL JUNCTION (3): This is the view from the down island platform looking towards Exeter on 7 May 1967 as Type 3 diesel No D6534 (later Class 33 No 33019) works the 9.00am Waterloo to Exeter service. This was the first down train to use the former up platform following singling. Nowadays the lines are signalled for either direction.**

On 12 January 2003 the GWR main line between Exeter and Taunton was closed and trains to and from Paddington were diverted via Yeovil Pen Mill and Junction. Some Waterloo to Exeter trains were terminated at Yeovil Junction and passengers transferred to trains from Paddington. Class 43 power car No 43025 heads the 'Cornish Riviera' into Yeovil Junction, while Class 159 No 159005 waits for passengers for Waterloo. *Ronald Lumber/TG*

YEOVIL JUNCTION (4): 'Schools' Class No 30913 *Christ's Hospital* stands at the head of the 11.04am train from Salisbury to Yeovil Town at Yeovil Junction on 8 August 1960.

Class 73 electro-diesels were very rarely seen west of Salisbury, but during the first week of October 1997 one worked an engineers' ballast train. It failed at Yeovil Junction and a second Class 73 was sent to its rescue. This also failed and the train remained at Yeovil Junction for more than a week! The two engines concerned were Nos 73104 and 73128. *Both TG*

YEOVIL JUNCTION (4): 'West Country' Class No 34108 *Wincanton* enters Yeovil Junction with a train of Bulleid coaches forming the 3.50pm Yeovil Town to Salisbury service on 9 August 1964.

Appalling weather on the night of 4 January 1998 resulted in the GWR main line being flooded at Staffords Bridge. The line was closed for about 48 hours, and trains from the Paddington line were diverted through Yeovil Pen Mill and Junction. The 03.00 from Dollands Moor to Exeter Riverside china clay empties, double-headed by Class 47 Nos 47200 *Herbert Austin* and 47241 *Halewood Silver Jubilee 1988*, approaches Yeovil Junction at first light the next morning. By this time there were also problems caused by bad weather on the LSWR main line. *Ronald Lumber/TG*

YEOVIL JUNCTION (5): Class 'S15' No 30844 has just passed through Yeovil Junction on an up express freight train to Nine Elms on 27 March 1961. The line curving away to the right is for Yeovil Town.

*Flying Scotsman* visited Yeovil Junction on 20 and 27 November 1999 and is seen here leaving for London on the second of these occasions with the 'Capital Scotsman'. In the left background is Class 47 No 47742 *The Enterprising Scot*. The excellent facilities of the South West Main Line Steam Company, which include an engine shed and turntable, attract several excursions to Yeovil every year. *Ronald Lumber/TG*

YEOVIL JUNCTION (6): Class 'U' No 31632 heads the 8.55am Ilfracombe to Waterloo away from Yeovil Junction on 8 August 1960. The station is on the extreme right, and the Weymouth to Yeovil Pen Mill line in the left foreground.

On a beautiful clear evening in July 2000 'West Country' Class No 34016 *Bodmin* heads for Woking with a special train. *Both TG*

**SHERBORNE (1):** The station is seen looking towards London on 10 May 1964. Little has changed here in the ensuing four decades, the only obvious differences being lifting barriers, an absence of up and down bays and a tastefully built extension to the main building. On 8 April 2003 Class 47 No 47734 *Crewe Diesel Depot* passes through Sherborne with the high-speed track-recording train on its way to Salisbury. *C. L. Caddy/TG*

**SHERBORNE (2): This much older photograph, taken in LSWR days, shows a double-headed down express entering the station.**

    **Steam is still seen at Sherborne, and on the evening of 15 April 2002 Bulleid 'Pacific' No 35005 *Canadian Pacific* passes the same point on the 'Cathedrals Express'.** *Lens of Sutton/TG*

**SHERBORNE (3): With a backdrop typical of north Dorset countryside, Class 50 No 50017 *Royal Oak* approaches Sherborne with the 09.10 train from Waterloo to Exeter St David's on 4 August 1991.**

    **On 15 March 2003 Class 5MT No 73096 heads for Exeter on a special train from Waterloo.** *Both TG*

SHERBORNE (4): Class 50 No 50041 *Bulwark* tackles the climb from Sherborne towards Templecombe on 12 August 1989 with the 11.05 train from Exeter St David's to Portsmouth & Southsea. Later in the day this engine worked a Portsmouth to Waterloo train before returning down the West of England main line.

Steam pounding up the bank makes an impressive sight, as witnessed on 6 July 2003. This is BR Standard 5MT No 73096 on the Yeovil Junction to London 'Cathedrals Express'. *Both TG*

SHERBORNE (5): Sister engine No 50030 *Repulse* takes the 11.10 train from Waterloo to Exeter St David's towards Sherborne on the same day as the previous 'past' photograph.

Trees now block photography on the down side of the line. On 21 June 2000 a weedkilling train is hauled by Class 37 No 37051 *Merehead* with unnamed No 37370 at the rear. The usual pattern for these trains was that they would run to Yeovil Junction, then to Weymouth and back via Pen Mill, before continuing to Exeter St David's. *Both TG*

BUCKHORN WESTON TUNNEL (1): 'Battle of Britain' Class No 34086 *219 Squadron* approaches the tunnel on an up express on 13 August 1964.

A train travelling in the opposite direction was photographed 39 years later. This is the track-recording train, top-and-tailed by Class 47 Nos 47734 *Crewe Diesel Depot* and 47772. The train is returning to Salisbury after running to Exeter. From Salisbury it will be routed via Virginia Water and Clapham Junction to Hither Green Depot. *Both TG*

**BUCKHORN WESTON TUNNEL (1):** Another 'Battle of Britain' 'Pacific', No 34077 *603 Squadron*, bursts out of the tunnel on the up 'Atlantic Coast Express' on 13 August 1964.

In contrast, 'Merchant Navy' Class No 35005 *Canadian Pacific* appears to exert little effort as it pulls the 'Cathedrals Express' over the summit on 17 April 2002. *Both TG*

GILLINGHAM: On 13 April 1964 the 4.35pm Exeter to Salisbury train was worked by Class 'S15' No 30833, fired from Yeovil Junction by Derek Phillips, in more recent years the author of several railway books.

Following completion of engineering works at Templecombe on 9 January 1999, Class 37 No 37717, with a train of redundant track panels, waits at Gillingham for a down service train to arrive. Down trains were terminated at Gillingham and passengers taken to Yeovil Junction by bus. *Both TG*

# INDEX OF LOCATIONS